CZERNY
PRACTICAL METHOD
FOR BEGINNERS
Opus 599

Edited and Recorded by Matthew Edwards

To access companion recorded performances online, visit:
www.halleonard.com/mylibrary

Enter Code
1219-4143-8320-9318

At the Piano (1876)
by Esther H. Jones
(1872–1916)
© Bourne Gallery, Reigate, Surrey/The Bridgeman Art Library

ISBN 978-1-61774-289-7

G. SCHIRMER, Inc.

DISTRIBUTED BY

7777 W. BLUEMOUND RD. P.O. BOX 13819 MILWAUKEE, WI 53213

www.musicsalesclassical.com
www.halleonard.com

CONTENTS

The price of this publication includes access to companion recorded performances online, for download or streaming, using the unique code found on the title page. Visit **www.halleonard.com/mylibrary** and enter the access code.

Melodies With and Without Ornaments (Nos. 71–100)

HISTORICAL NOTES

CARL CZERNY (1791–1857)

Although born into a rather humble family with few prospects of prosperity or good education, Carl Czerny is today a household name, well-known to pianists around the world. Through good fortune, and a degree of talent, he interacted with some of the most important names in both Classical and Romantic literature. The list of his contacts is nearly unbelievable: he studied with Beethoven and Clementi; taught Liszt, Thalberg, and Leschetizky; and associated with countless others including Chopin, Constanze Mozart (Mozart's wife), Franz Xaver Süssmayer (Mozart's pupil), Andreas Streicher (the piano manufacturer), and many more. He was the first—or at least one of the first—to perform many of Beethoven's works, and wrote original compositions of such popularity in his day, that publishers were willing to print anything he submitted. Very often, they did not even care to hear or see it before the contract was signed.

Without doubt, Czerny lived in interesting times, and was privileged to observe first-hand the transition from the Classicism of Haydn and Mozart to the passion of the Romantics. Of course, none other than Ludwig van Beethoven was his guide through this most significant progression. Czerny stood as an observer at the crossroads of these two styles, but he also saw—and, to a great degree, assisted in—the transformation of keyboard technique. By the combination of the fame of his publications, and his successful teaching career, he became one of the foremost authorities on piano playing during this time. Even today, his legacy is sustained by his multiple collections of exercises and pedagogical works. Though his life is primarily summarized by these, a thorough study would reveal a man of many skills and interests.

Czerny's grandfather had been a violinist, and his father, Wenzel Czerny (1750–1832), played several instruments, including piano, organ, and oboe. Wenzel did not marry until 1786, delayed by his fifteen years of service in the army.[1] Carl, who would be the couple's only child, was born in Vienna, Austria, on February 21, 1791. The family briefly moved to Poland, but returned to Vienna in 1795, where his father began a moderately successful career of piano teaching and piano maintenance.

It is no surprise, then, that Carl was attracted to the piano early on; his autobiography states that he began playing at the age of three, and by seven was also composing.[2] His parents kept him close to home, generally removed from most of his would-be playmates, providing ample opportunity for his musical interests. In addition, much of his education came from his father's piano students, who, as part of their lesson fees, tutored Carl in a variety of subjects including French, German, and literature. Yet about this relative isolation, he states that he "never missed the friendship of other boys, and never went out without my father."[3]

His father's skill as a pianist and teacher was at least good enough to give young Carl an excellent foundation in technique and sight-reading. He describes it thus:

> My father had no intention whatever of making a superficial virtuoso out of me; rather, he strove to develop my sight-reading ability through continuous study of new works and thus to develop my musicianship. When I was barely ten I was already able to play cleanly and fluently nearly everything by Mozart, Clementi, and the other piano composers of the time; owing to my excellent musical memory I mostly performed without the music. Whatever money my father could set aside from the scant pay for his lessons was spent on music for me…[4]

Perhaps the critical moment in the life of Carl Czerny was his introduction to Beethoven. One of Beethoven's closest friends was a man named Wenzel Krumpholz, who also happened to be a friend of the Czerny family. Through Krumpholz, Carl became aware of the great composer, and as soon as he was able, began playing as much of his music as he could find. Impressed by the 10-year old's pianism and musicality, Krumpholz agreed to take the boy and his father to Beethoven's home for a formal introduction.

The apartment was high above the street, and was rather unkempt and disheveled. Other musicians were there rehearsing, but they quickly became an impromptu audience for Carl as he sat down at Beethoven's piano to play. He performed the first movement of Mozart's C major piano concerto (K. 503), and Beethoven's own recently released Pathétique Sonata. When he finished, Beethoven uttered the words that quite possibly set Czerny's future success in motion: "The boy is talented, I myself want to teach him, and I accept him as my pupil. Let him come several times a week."[5]

Although the lessons lasted little more than a year due to Beethoven's growing need to focus on composition and the Czernys' financial situation, the relationship continued to grow until Beethoven's death in 1827. Czerny often worked closely with him, even writing the piano reduction for the publication of *Fidelio*. He also taught piano to Beethoven's nephew Carl, and gave widely successful early performances of Beethoven's works.

Performing never took a central role in Czerny's career—in fact, he cancelled his very first concert tour in 1805 even though it was supported by Beethoven himself![6] Instead, he turned his attention to teaching and composing, and found significant success in both areas. For many years, he taught twelve hours daily, and, by means of his prominent reputation, was able to charge very well for the instruction. While it was common for him to teach many of the most talented young people of the day, at least one eclipsed them all. Czerny describes the first meeting like this:

One morning in 1819… a man brought a small boy about eight years of age to me and asked me to let that little fellow play for me. He was a pale, delicate-looking child and while playing swayed on the chair as if drunk so that I often thought he would fall to the floor. Moreover, his playing was completely irregular, careless, and confused, and he had so little knowledge of correct fingering that he threw his fingers over the keyboard in an altogether arbitrary fashion. Nevertheless, I was amazed by the talent with which Nature had equipped him.[7]

Rarely does one hear such a dismal description of the great Franz Liszt, but such was Czerny's first impression. Over the next fourteen months, he worked with the boy every evening, requiring him to learn rapidly and work tirelessly on technical exercises including Czerny's own works.[8]

If we combine Czerny's published and unpublished works, his compositions number more than 1,000. He wrote symphonies, variations, arrangements, chamber works, and sacred choral works in addition to his numerous pedagogical works. Not all of his music was received well—in particular, Schumann's review of a piano work entitled *The Four Seasons* stated that "it would be hard to discover a greater bankruptcy in imagination than Czerny has proved."[9] Harsh, to be sure, but many of the greatest pianists, including Liszt and Chopin, played his works throughout the continent, to great acclaim. To this day, many of the sonatas are regularly performed.

Professionally, Czerny's reputation remained generally high throughout his life. Personally, however, he remained alone, never marrying. His brief autobiography, which describes his life to 1842, ends rather abruptly with the following sentence: "In 1827 I lost my mother and five years later (1832) my father, and was thus left all alone, since I have no relatives whatever."

Carl Czerny died on July 15, 1857. A humble beginning, a quiet passing; but in between, a remarkable life.

PERFORMANCE NOTES

Introduction to Czerny's Music

Czerny organized his compositions for piano into four main categories:

- Studies and exercises
- Easy pieces for students
- Brilliant pieces for concerts
- Serious music[10]

He is best known for his pedagogical and technical works, yet he also wrote many compositional treatises. He seems to have held to the idea that performance and composition should go hand in hand, and even expressed disappointment that Liszt had not had sufficient instruction from him in composition.[11] He was a pedagogue at heart, and sought through all of his works to teach and admonish young musicians.

Practical Method for Beginners on the Pianoforte, Op. 599

This particular set of exercises is one of his most popular collections. Other prominent pedagogical books include 100 Progressive Studies for the Piano, Op. 139 and The Little Pianist, Op. 823; the latter intended to be a true method book for beginners. More difficult etudes can be found in The School of Velocity, Op. 299 and The Art of Finger Dexterity, Op. 740. There are many more etudes and exercises, but these are some of the best known.

Czerny gave many of these works to his students, with the intent of perfecting and polishing their technique. Indeed, many who heard Liszt play before and after Czerny's lessons credited the intense study of these (and other) etudes as the source of Liszt's flawless virtuosity. With such a recommendation, it would be unwise to ignore these works.

General Suggestions

This publication should be approached with purpose; it is not meant to be simply a required element of lessons, or a set of mundane "drills" to add an extra few minutes onto practice time. The goal for each exercise should be to learn good technique and fundamental musicality. Speed is at all times secondary to these two items. With the proper attention to good technique, speed will follow on its own.

I frequently mention technique in my commentary on the individual pieces, and have attempted to clarify certain approaches to the keyboard that have proven extremely useful to me and to my students. However, it is understandably difficult to convey the subtleties of piano technique in just a few words.

Clarity and Evenness

The pieces in this publication should be played clearly and evenly. It is typically a sign of a technical problem if there is an unexpected accent or rhythmic unevenness in a scale or arpeggio. It is most important, in order to overcome this problem, that the fingers and hand (and by extension, the entire body) stay relaxed; by tensing your muscles, everything becomes more difficult. In addition, focusing on this element trains the ear to listen carefully, and encourages good practice habits.

Fingering

Remember that the fingerings given here are suggestions only. Every hand is different, so every fingering should be examined; don't try to force a fingering that may not work for you!

Generally, I have tried to follow a few principles for my fingering choices:
- A relaxed hand: In the majority of cases, I have tried to keep the fingers close together, and the hand moving as a unit. This more easily allows the fingers to stay relaxed, and the hand to move both faster and more smoothly. Of course, stretches are required when extending to the octave and beyond (or the sixth, for smaller hands), but allow the hand to move toward the extended note, keeping the fingers relaxed.

- Economy of motion: this applies to the fingers alone, as well as to the entire hand. Simply put, it is the idea of minimizing the number of crossovers in a passage—grouping as many notes into one hand position as possible. Imagine for example, if a simple C major arpeggio over three octaves were played with only the first and second fingers; there would be several hand positions, creating a much more difficult passage.

Tempos

Metronome markings are not included in the majority of printed editions, and I have chosen not to recommend any specific tempos here. The primary focus of this edition should be the improvement of technique, and learning how to deal with certain technical issues—both pianistic and physical. I have seen too many students practice for hours, pursuing a metronomic goal with tunnel vision, ignoring the fact that their physical approach may not ever allow them to achieve top speed.

Indeed, this is not to say that fast tempos should be avoided, by any means. Rather, they must be approached carefully. Consider the recording as a suggested tempo, but by no means the exact tempo for every student. Each student should play the faster pieces as quickly and as cleanly as good technique will allow.

Ornamentation

> The graces, namely, the shake, the turn, the appoggiatura, etc., are the flowers of music; and the clear, correct, and delicate execution of them, embellishes and exalts every melody and every passage. But, when they are played stiff, hard, or unintelligibly, they may rather be compared to blots of ink or spots of dirt.[12]

A great deal of research and opinion are available on this topic. While it is important to be familiar with the current conventional wisdom, one cannot forget the fundamental principle that ornaments, as Czerny himself said above, are decorative and improvisatory. They are decorative in the sense that they are subservient to the primary line, and improvisatory in that their execution varies—slightly or greatly—from performer to performer. In the Baroque era, J.S. Bach wrote a very detailed chart, explaining the ornamentation written in his works. However, Sandra Rosenblum, in her extremely helpful book *Performance Practices in Classic Piano Music* states that "Neither Haydn, Mozart, nor Beethoven left

any systematic instructions for the performance of ornaments."[13] Clementi is perhaps the most significant composer to write instructions on ornamentation, yet Rosenblum further states that "Although many treatises discussed ornaments and gave instructions for their performance, there was not—and is not now—complete agreement regarding either notation or performance."[14] The point to be seen here is that while there may be some general "rules" about the execution of turns, trills, and appoggiaturas, there are still many valid variables left to the unique and instinctive choice of each performer.

Musicality

These works are miniature creations, and by the simple fact of their brevity, do not contain excessively deep musical thoughts. However, they can be used to learn countless basic principles, such as shaping a line, closing a phrase, planning the dynamic architecture of a work, and of course, following the printed markings. Strive to make each piece as musical as possible.

Notes on Selected Exercises

Nos. 1–10: First Exercises for Learning the Notes

A single glance at these first ten "note-learning" exercises will show that they are considerably different from today's methods. While many would feel they are too complex and difficult for the absolute beginner, at the very least these exercises could be attempted early in a student's keyboard education.

While one should be generally cautious about excessive finger numbering in beginning literature, as it may cause a student to rely on the number more than the notation, they may be genuinely useful in these early exercises. Rather quickly, the hands stray from a standard five-finger position, hopefully avoiding the idea that Middle C = 1.

Exercises 1–4
These first works are excellent for teaching and reinforcing the basics: rounded fingers, legato touch, and dynamics that follow the rise and fall of the line.

Exercises 5–7
As the range opens up wider over larger intervals, focus on maintaining the roundness of the fingers. This will require moving the fingers (and hand) TO each note, rather than stretching the fingers widely, causing tension.

Exercises 8–10

Chords are introduced here, and the emphasis should continue to be rounded fingers and a relaxed hand position. Encourage students to avoid "grabbing" each chord, as if pulling something out of the piano, but rather "setting" the chord into the keys, as if setting a tennis ball on a table.

Nos. 11–18: Five-Finger Exercises With Quiet Hand

These exercises help to develop independence of the hands, with several of them requiring one hand to be more "still" than the other. Independence of the hands is the first critical step in learning to voice the melody clearly over the harmony.

The number of finger markings is dramatically decreased at this point, and are used only to suggest a suitable method of playing. One point to make is about fingerings on repeated notes. A common suggestion in this situation is to play each repeated note with a different finger, as in 3-2-1, etc. However, I suggested in several situations to use the same finger for the repeated notes, particularly when the repetition is brief, or the tempo is not quick. I often will use a fingering like this in the event that alternating fingerings prove to be more awkward.

Lastly, throughout this set, the right hand remains in a fairly close position; this will help to maintain a good rounded and relaxed hand position.

Exercises 11–12 and 17–18

These works contain predominantly triads, often in whole notes, in the left hand. The emphasis should be on maintaining a gentler sound in the left hand, while focusing on the melodic shaping of the right. In addition, after the chord is played, allow the hand to stay relaxed, even while holding the notes down.

One practice suggestion for acquiring the independence of the hands through these particular exercises is to practice "playing" the chords with no sound at all, while the other hand plays normally. To do this, allow the left hand to touch the correct notes, without actually depressing them down into the keybed. As confidence and understanding grows from this, allow the chords to become gradually louder, until a proper balance of melody and harmony is reached.

Number 17 is a good early study for double thirds in a single hand. In particular, the repeated thirds in measures 7, 9, etc. encourage a flexible wrist, which is an important part of any double thirds passagework. Use number 14 as a preparation.

In number 18, try to make the right hand as melodic as possible, stretching across the barlines to the end of measures 8 and 16.

Exercises 13 and 15–16

A slight variation on the other exercises in this section, here the left hand is required to hold a single whole note, while playing the remainder of the chord in quarters. Again, it is important to hold the whole note without tension, so that the quarters will be even and dynamically balanced under the melody.

Exercise 14

The first of many "Alberti bass" accompaniments in this book, this also serves as a preparation for the double thirds of number 17, as stated above. Be sure that the thirds are played exactly together, with the weight balanced in the center of each interval.

Nos. 19–26: First Exercises for the Thumb

Scales and some arpeggiated passages are the predominant theme in this section. If the student has begun to achieve a consistently relaxed and rounded hand from the previous exercises, then learning to cross over will be much easier. The thumb (when descending) or the finger (when ascending) cannot be thought of as a "pivot-point," which rotates on the note itself, causing the elbow to swing out away from the body, and yet still often requires the finger to stretch for the next note. Another variant of this is when students attempt to twist at the wrist for the crossover. Far less motion is involved when the hand, while traveling up or down the keyboard, moves forward a bit at the point of the crossover, allowing the finger or thumb plenty of room to comfortably find the next note. This approach to crossing also is better for avoiding accents or rhythmic "bumps" at the point of the crossover.

Exercise 19

Keep the left hand well under the right hand dynamically, supporting the melody.

Exercise 20

A very slight emphasis on the lowest left hand note in each measure will help to make the harmony clear. Keep this bass figure generally soft, and shape the right hand melody through its peaks and valleys. Remember not to let the repeated quarters be static, but give them dynamic direction toward the next pitch.

Exercises 21 and 24

Continue focusing on a rounded hand for the double thirds, but try to balance the hand slightly in favor of the upper note, so as to bring out the melody more clearly.

Exercise 22

While this is an excellent exercise for right-hand passagework, it is also a good study for the left hand. Keep the repeated thirds light, almost moving forward with each note, rather than sinking too deeply into the keybed each time.

Exercise 23

When the accompaniment contains a note on each beat, a bit more concentration is needed to keep it below the melody. Generally, the melody should be very legato and lyrical, with the left hand providing a smooth, unbroken harmony.

Exercise 25

Don't let these chords be too harsh! Practice first by playing only the top note of the right hand, to hear the melody alone. Next, add the remaining notes, and try to shape it the same way, leaning the balance toward the top note for good voicing.

Exercise 26

A slight accent on beat one will give this work a good sense of forward motion and energy.

Nos. 27–31: Exercises Exceeding an Octave

Exercise 27

Keep the left hand light and the right hand steady; sometimes, sixteenth notes in close repeating patterns can become uneven. Even if parts of this seem easy to play fast, always be sure that every single note is heard clearly.

Exercise 28

Even over these larger distances in the right hand, keep the fingers rounded, and as relaxed as possible; in particular, don't let the fifth finger stretch out flatly.

Exercise 29

The meter of this should feel clearly in two, with each beat gently pushing forward to the beginning of the next measure. Be sure repeated notes are not dynamically flat.

Exercise 30

Hold the left hand dotted half down gently, so that the other notes can be played freely. The main motive of the right hand contains a two-note slur, which sounds lovely here when played with the traditional "strong-weak" dynamic. Be sure that the sixteenth-note scales near the end match the same lyrical quality of the opening.

Exercise 31

Focus on the voicing of these slightly larger intervals in the right hand. Listen carefully to the left hand, keeping the fingers round and relaxed so that the triplets don't play too close together. Drop the fifth finger into the keys; "grabbing" the notes will likely cause the first two notes to actually play at the same time.

Nos. 32–35: Exercises With the Bass Clef

Exercises 32 and 35

Carefully voice and shape the chords in the right hand and keep the left hand lively. Perhaps the hands can be a bit more equal here, as the literal distance between the hands helps to separate them in our ears.

Exercise 33

Focus on keeping the sixteenth notes clear and even, particularly when the hands are playing in unison.

Exercise 34

Use the suggested fingering to make the upper note of the sixths as legato as possible. In measures 13–15 the fingering requires a crossover while playing thirds; keep the thumb in contact with the lower note as the upper finger crosses over to give a bit of legato to the passage.

Nos. 36–38: Exercises With Sharps and Flats

A general suggestion for this small group of exercises is to focus on moving the hand to the black notes, rather than stretching the finger out flatly and awkwardly. Moving to the note allows the finger to remain rounded.

Exercise 36

When the accompaniment is low, and therefore naturally louder, as in the beginning of this exercise, pay special attention to keeping the melody above it dynamically. Be careful not to accent the accidentals.

Exercise 37
Work carefully on keeping the double-note passages legato; also avoid accenting when a crossover is required.

Exercise 38
This exercise has a slightly mischievous sound to it; keep it light, with good accents where marked.

Nos. 39–42: Exercises in Other Easy Keys

Czerny begins introducing other key signatures in this set, starting with G major and F major. Additional sharps and flats will follow throughout the course of the book.

Exercise 39
This exercise has a lyrical melody with a very natural rise and fall. Be sure the *forte* marking at measure 12 is the peak moment.

Exercise 40
Staccato and legato markings are closely mixed in this work; be sure the staccatos are not accented, so as not to break the shape of the line.

Exercise 41
Nearly the opposite of the preceding exercise, the focus here is lyricism. Keep the left hand notes flowing gently under the right hand.

Exercise 42
A slower and more stately tempo requires more work to keep the melodic line connected, and properly shaped. Imagine singing or playing this melody on a wind instrument to help bridge the gap between the notes.

Nos. 43–57: Exercises With Rests

Not every one of these exercises deal particularly with rests, yet Czerny gives no other category of exercise until number 58. Those that do deal with rests specifically seem to be a study in the timely release of notes. Additionally, some of the works, through the use of the rests, allow both hands to alternate in importance.

Exercise 43
Keep this work bright and energetic by following the rests carefully. Several of the chords can be staccato, providing at times a nice contrast to the legato portions of the melody.

Exercise 44
Again, light and bright for this exercise. Keep the wrist flexible, so as not become too harsh in the

sound. Be sure the right hand repeated notes are moving dynamically toward the next measure.

Exercise 45
Don't allow the staccatos to be accented, particularly after the pair of sixteenths, as in the first measure. Practice measures 21–24 carefully, as it is the first significant left-hand sixteenth-note passage in the book.

Exercise 46
Emphasize the contrast between legato and staccato, whether the contrast exists within a single hand (mm. 1–4), or between the two hands, (mm. 17–20). In a way, this is an extension of the concept of independence of the hands, and provides a good study for that.

Exercise 47
The crossovers here are a bit larger, encompassing a third on multiple occasions. Treat these essentially the same as when crossing only a half or whole step, avoiding a large elbow movement, or twisting at the wrist. A rounded hand will make this much easier.

Exercise 48
Keep the wrist flexible for the repeated thirds and sixths. Staccatos should be light and sharp to better contrast with the phrase markings.

Exercise 49
Don't think of this as simply a scale exercise; make the right hand as melodic as possible.

Exercise 50
Work for a very long, smooth line in the left hand, closing the phrases exactly where indicated. The lyrical nature of this line makes it equal in importance to the right hand. In the second half, be sure to voice the top note of the right hand thirds.

Exercise 51
Multiple items are studied in this little exercise. First, the dotted eighth-sixteenth pattern is introduced; as always, care should be taken to execute the rhythm precisely, not allowing it to slow into a sort of triplet figure. In the second half, keep the left hand very legato, as marked, under the sharper right hand staccatos.

Exercise 52
This piece is an opportunity for slower, expressive music-making. Be sure to lean toward the tops of

the right hand intervals and chords, to bring out the melody. Also, be sure to give some small musical shape to the left hand phrases, treating them as if the two hands are having a conversation.

Exercise 53

This brisk-tempo exercise is another opportunity to practice legato in the right hand, and staccato in the left. Make sure the chords follow the dynamic line of the right hand.

Exercise 54

This should be played as a slow, graceful waltz. Be careful to shape the line even when it is not marked as legato.

Exercise 55

In places such as the first measure, play the sixteenth note after the dotted eighth as part of the melodic line, not as a brief ornament preceding the next "real" note of the melody. Notice also the longer notes in the left hand in measures 13–15, to emphasize the harmonic motion.

Exercise 56

Keep the thumb relaxed, so that these chromatic scales are as smooth and even as possible. Also, continue the musical line when the ascent (or descent) turns into staccato eighth notes.

Exercise 57

The fingerings here are suggested in order to keep the hand in only two distinct positions for the opening figure, and similar figures. In this way, the hand only moves once to play all four beats. Be sure the tempo feels like a bright two.

Nos. 58–70: Exercises to Attain Velocity

Certainly the previous exercises were not intended to be played at a snail's pace, but for this set, speed and agility become the primary technique for Czerny. Throughout these exercises, always focus on a rounded and relaxed hand, on moving the hand and fingers to the notes, and on avoiding any awkward or unnatural movements.

Exercise 58–60

Similar in principle to Hanon numbers 5 and 6, there is a lot of trill and tremolo-type motion here. Practice an octave tremolo for the right hand, and gradually decrease it by steps until the distance is a third, and later a second. Try to maintain the same kind of back-and-forth rotation as the interval gets smaller, then use this skill when learning the right hand. Number 59 moves the study to the left hand, and number 60 puts both hands to work on this technique. For this last exercise, keep the hand slightly more open for the larger intervals, yet still relaxed.

Exercise 61

Further practice on the smooth crossing of thumbs and fingers. Keep the hand moving consistently in the direction of the scale, and relaxed to avoid rhythmic bumps.

Exercise 62

The most common problem in triplet accompaniments such as those found here is the grouping or "clumping" together of two or more notes. Most times, this is caused by "grabbing" the lower left-hand or higher right-hand notes with the upper three fingers. In the case of the left hand, drop the fifth finger into the key, feeling completely separate from the other fingers.

Exercise 63

The triplets here provide a beautiful rising and falling line for what would otherwise simply be scales. Be sure to keep the fingers relaxed as the figures change, as in measures 13–16.

Exercise 64

A true and exciting scherzo, keep the left hand light, and supportive. In measure 17, treat this figure exactly as if it were a tremolo between the highest and lowest note. Don't allow the additional note to cause any tension, but balance the two fingers over the center of the interval, as one unit.

Exercises 65 and 67

Again, think of these trills as very small tremolos, using the exercise described under number 58 as a warm-up. The rotation is the same, spread over a much smaller distance. The left hand trills of number 67 may prove a bit more difficult; at first, it may help to try a different pair of fingers for each measure.

Exercise 66

The left hand measures contain dotted half notes, to sustain the bass note of the harmony. This is a good chance to focus on further independence of the hands, as the left must be less energetic than the right. More tremolo work for the right hand at measure 9, with the melody resting on top of the figure; work carefully to shape that melody, as if it were alone.

Exercise 68

When changing the fingers for these repeated note patterns, allow the hand to move very slightly forward over the note with each successive finger, rather than grabbing at it—almost with the motion of snapping your fingers. For the figure in measure 17, this forward motion will have to restart after each time the thumb plays. Work carefully to avoid unnecessary accents.

Exercise 69

Focus on clarity more than speed. Since most of the scales are a single octave in length, these passages each are a single, rising gesture; excellent practice for clarity and relaxed speed.

Exercise 70

Be sure these scales in octaves and tenths are even, and precisely together.

Nos. 71–100: Melodies With and Without Ornaments

This is the last titled section in the book, and it is unclear if Czerny actually intended all of the last 30 exercises to be under the same heading. At the very least, 71–83 seem most appropriate for the category. The remaining works continue to emphasize topics previously covered.

Given the emphasis on melody, this section also contains generally slower tempo indications. This should provide ample opportunity to practice good tone and depth of sound.

As for the ornamented pieces, the primary exercise is to make these sound very natural, unaccented, and genuinely decorative. See the notes above for more details on ornaments.

Exercise 71

Deep tone, and a well-shaped line will make this a lovely work. Consider also the half notes in the left hand, emphasizing the harmonic counterpoint between the hands.

Exercise 72

At the Allegretto tempo, this piece should be very graceful. Many of the cadences conclude on beat two or three, giving the resolution a gentler sound, so be sure not to accent the final chord.

Exercises 73, 76 and 81

It is most important that the ornaments enhance the musical line, not detract from it through overstated accents or sudden bursts of attention-grabbing speed. A good first example is the grace note in measure 7 of number 73; its dynamic should be in the context of the line, gently and without surprise. The other ornaments should follow the same basic principle.

In number 81, be sure to give direction to the repeated notes of the melody.

Exercise 74

The trills and their conclusions should be relaxed and not *agitato*. The turns at measure 6 sound the most natural if they are played on the beat, although nothing indicates that they cannot be played before the beat.

Exercise 75

Be careful not to accent beat one of measure 2 too strongly; it is the natural "goal" of the ornament. Also, treat the ornament after the trills (measure 17, etc.) as part of the line leading to the high note, rather than just a quick conclusion of the trill.

Exercise 77

For the opening arpeggio, choose the fingering that makes the smoothest line. Be sure again to make the grace notes decorative.

Exercise 78

The focus here is the voicing and shaping of a melody that is at the top of a chord. Leaning the hand and weight slightly to the top will make this easier. However, keep the other voices in mind, especially when they are moving, so that this work takes on a chorale-like sound.

Exercise 79

Be sure to give the tied notes a very slight accent, so that the sound carries into the next measure. Holding the left hand dotted quarters will ensure that the downbeat remains clear.

Exercises 80 and 82

The triplets in these works are almost like written-out ornaments; while all of the notes contribute to the line, some of the notes (often those landing right on beats one and three) seem to be more important. These should not necessarily be accented, but an awareness of this will help in following the harmony. The triplets at measure 25 of number 80 are a bit more difficult, as they need to sound like a line, and not two ornaments.

It may be appropriate to give a sharper or brighter character to the grace notes in number 82; a slight accent here contributes to the bright mood of this piece.

Exercise 83
To shape a line over rests such as these, one must mentally sing the melody; otherwise, they will sound dull and flat. Allow the left hand to help with the crescendo and decrescendo. Larger grace notes are presented here, but they should be treated the same as more common ones.

Exercise 84
Generally, the difficult aspect of arpeggio playing is the crossover; without careful practice, the rhythm can be disrupted, or unwanted accents can be inserted. Focus on making the crossover smooth by staying relaxed with the two fingers (and/or thumb) involved. Remember to keep the hand constantly moving in the direction of the arpeggio, not locked into a single position.

Exercise 85
To keep the right hand rhythmic figure steady, be sure to keep the left hand absolutely on beat. By focusing on the notes that are on the strong beat, those that are off the beat tend to fall more naturally into place.

Exercise 86
The triplets are accompanimental, yet they should help carry the dynamic shape of the melody. In the right hand, be sure not to accent any notes that come right before a leap to a new register, as in measure 3. In a sense, don't worry about the low note until you have played the current note exactly as it should be.

Exercise 87
This exercise offers plenty of practice for careful choreography of the arpeggios. As stated for number 84, keep the hand moving, and don't "grab" any notes with the thumb.

Exercise 88
Watch the articulation and fingerings here carefully. Keep the hand rounded for the double notes, in particular when the register changes quickly, as in measure 9.

Exercises 89–90
These exercises are more about broken four-note chords than about arpeggios. Because the span is only an octave, it can be tempting to simply grab

them all, creating tension in the hand. A better alternative is to keep the hand round, as if the "arpeggio" were literally only four notes long. In number 89, measures 1–7, don't lose or accent the last note of the figure; this is often caused by concern for reaching down to the next note, even though it is usually only an octave. By staying relaxed all the way to the top, the move down will be much easier.

Exercise 91
Another excellent exercise for double thirds, this introduces the crossover, in preparation for double third scales. Yet again, focus on the smooth transition of the crossover. Do not tense up, or the rhythm will be affected. Keep the hand light, and the wrist supple.

Exercise 92
Keep the thumb and second finger relaxed as they arrive at the trill on beat three. Similarly, in measure 9, beginning the arpeggios with a relaxed fifth finger will help it to be smoother.

Exercises 93–94
Both of these exercises combine scales and arpeggios for the right hand. Let the hand move naturally over the contour of the passages, keeping it rounded above the keys, and not flat against them.

Exercise 95
There are two distinct ornaments here, and there should be a slight difference in how they are played. On the recording, the ornament in measure 1 is played before the beat, while the one in measure 11 is played on the beat. See the discussion about ornamentation in the notes above.

Exercise 96
Follow the fingering for the fewest number of hand position changes. Also, allow the hand/wrist to rotate for each pair of intervals, in the same way as a tremolo, for measures 1–7.

Exercises 97
Czerny clearly indicates that these ornaments should be played directly on the first beat, which makes for a more *marcato* sound. Contrast those chords with a very legato triplet line. At measure 9, be sure not to accent the eighth note, as the hand moves up/down to the next register.

Exercise 98
Even though the notes of the trill are only a step apart, play them with rotation similar to

an octave tremolo. Keep a relaxed hand as they are played; tightening the hand and forcing the fingers to trill will only make the muscles tired, and the trills uneven.

Exercise 99
For measures 1, 5, and 6, focus on keeping the hands precisely in unison.

Exercise 100
The fingering in measures 1 and 3 may at first seem a bit awkward, but it can make a very smooth arpeggio if played with a relaxed hand. Whenever the thumb does play a black note in this piece, be sure not to accent it unnecessarily.

NOTES

1 Little is known about his mother—she is described by Czerny simply as "a Moravian girl."
2 Czerny, Carl. "Recollections from My Life." Trans. Ernest Sanders. *The Musical Quarterly*, Vol. 42, No. 3. (Jul., 1956), p. 303.
3 ibid., 305.
4 ibid., 303.
5 ibid., 307.
6 Stephan D. Lindeman and George Barth, "Czerny, Carl," *Grove Music Online*, ed. Laura Macy: www.grovemusic.com (accessed 1 Feb. 2011).
7 Czerny, Carl. "Recollections from My Life." Trans. Ernest Sanders. *The Musical Quarterly*, Vol. 42, No. 3. (Jul., 1956), pp. 314–315.
8 Alan Walker, et al, "Liszt, Franz." *Grove Music Online*, ed. Laura Macy: www.grovemusic.com (accessed 1 Feb. 2011).
9 Stephan D. Lindeman and George Barth, "Czerny, Carl," *Grove Music Online*, ed. Laura Macy: www.grovemusic.com (accessed 1 Feb. 2011).
10 ibid.
11 Czerny, Carl. "Recollections from My Life." Trans. Ernest Sanders. *The Musical Quarterly*, Vol. 42, No. 3. (Jul., 1956), p. 316.
12 Czerny, Carl. *Letters to a Young Lady, on the Art of Playing the Pianoforte.* Trans. J. A. Hamilton. (Da Capo Press: New York), 1982.
13 Rosenblum, Sandra. *Performance Practices in Classic Piano Music* (Indiana University Press: Bloomington, 1988), p. 216.
14 ibid., p. 217.

Practical Method for Beginners on the Piano

First Exercises for Learning the Notes

Carl Czerny
Op. 599

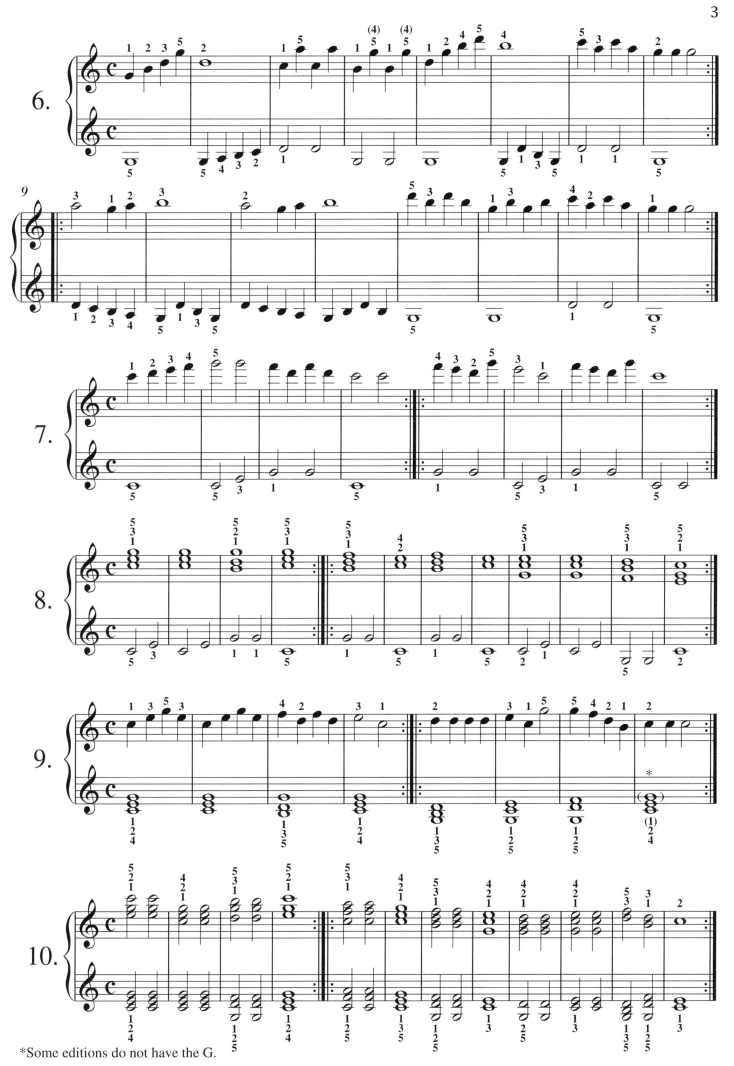

*Some editions do not have the G.

Five-Finger Exercises With Quiet Hand

First Exercises for the Thumb

Exercises Exceeding an Octave

Exercises With the Bass Clef

* Some editions print F instead of G in the right hand.

Exercises With Sharps and Flats

Exercises in Other Easy Keys

Exercises with Rests

Allegro moderato

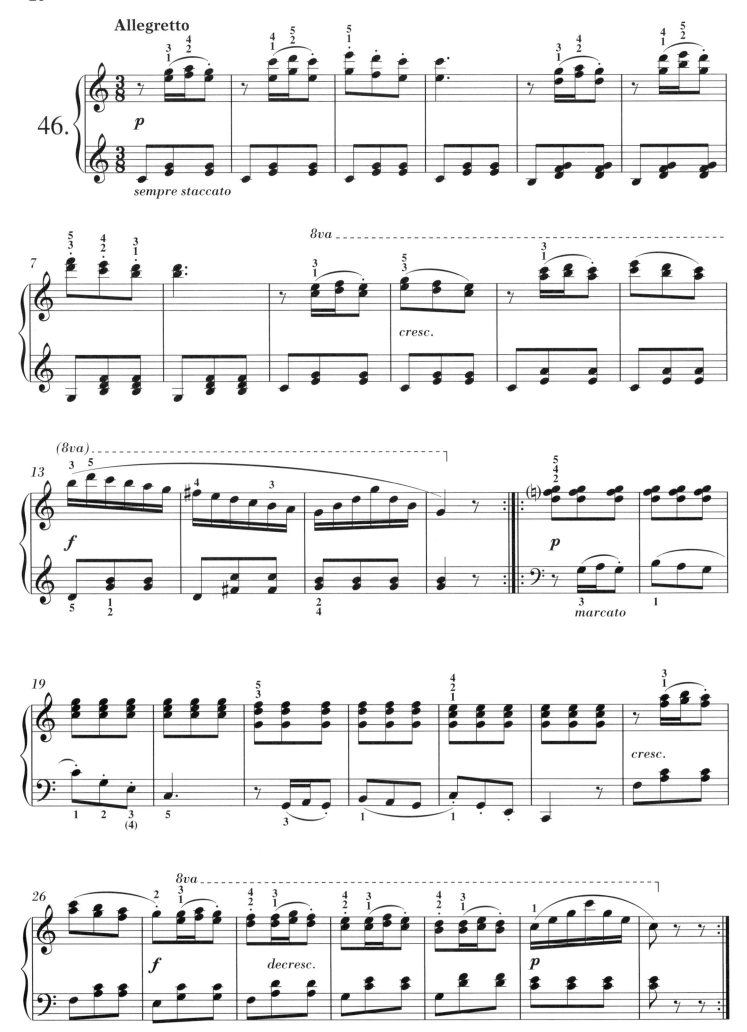

Fine

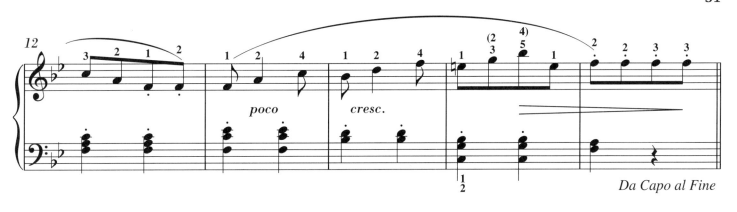

Da Capo al Fine

Moderato

54.

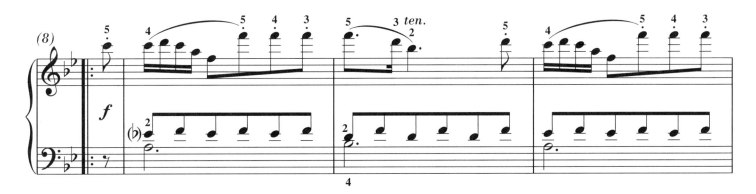

Allegro

Da Capo al Fine

Exercises to Attain Velocity

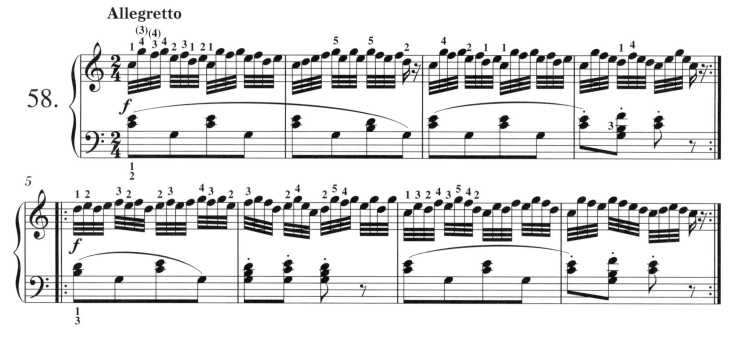

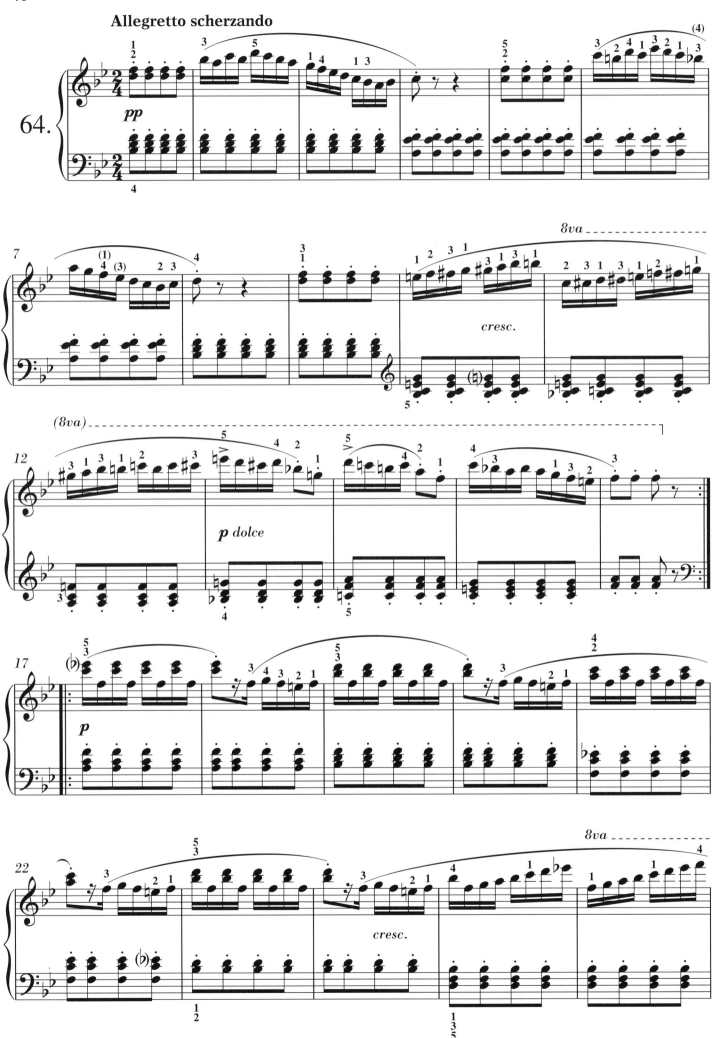

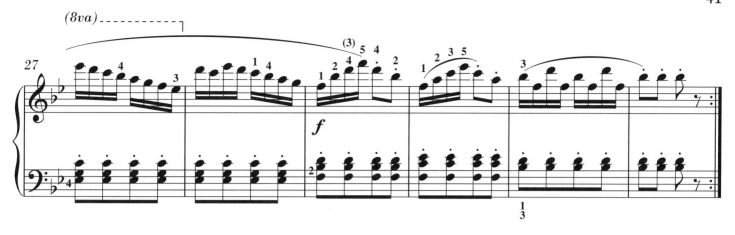

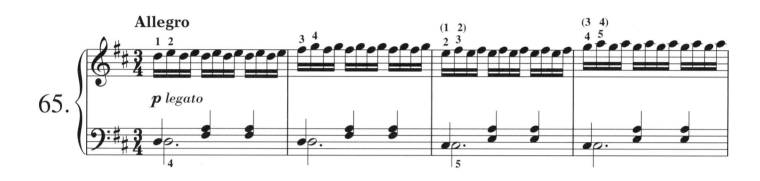

65.

Allegretto

69.

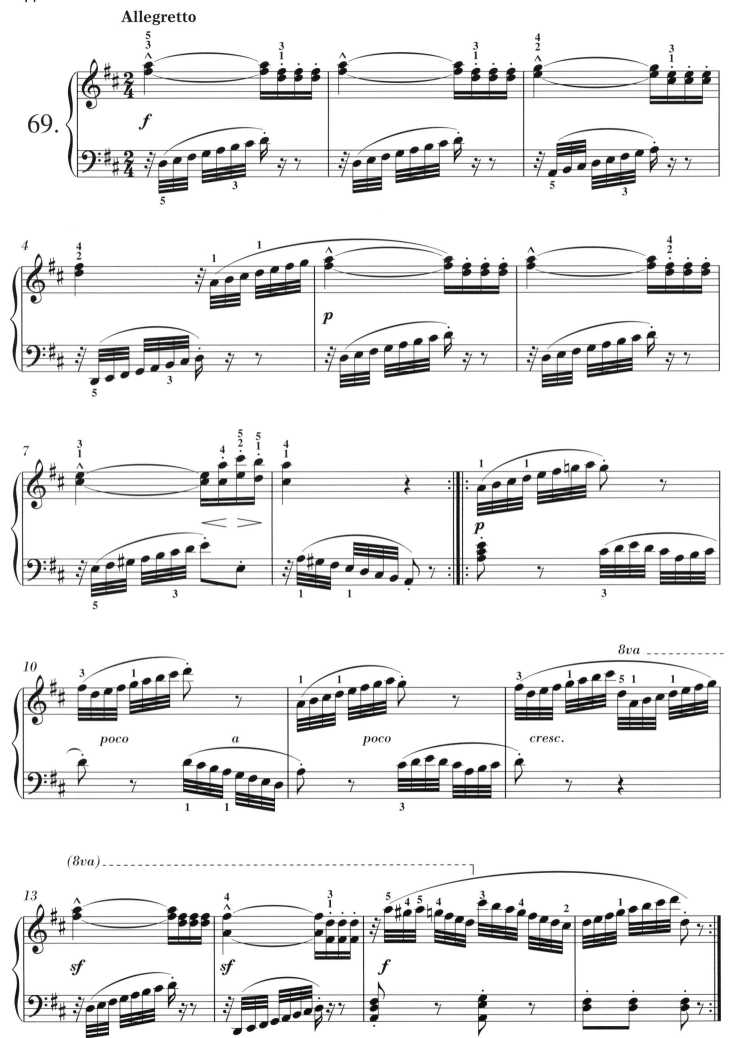

Melodies With and Without Ornaments

Andantino

74.

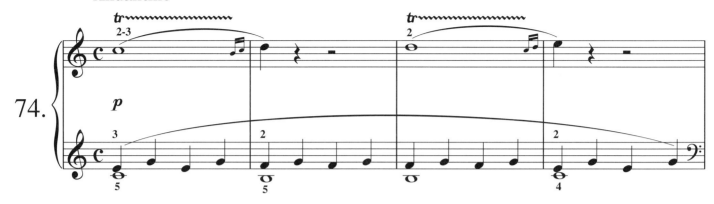

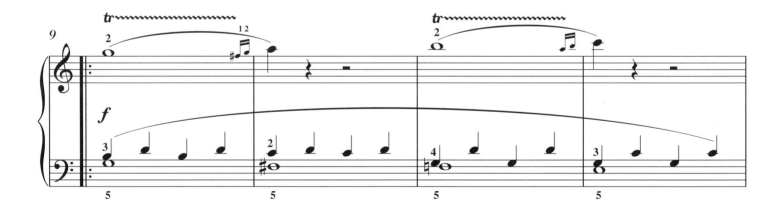

Allegretto

76.

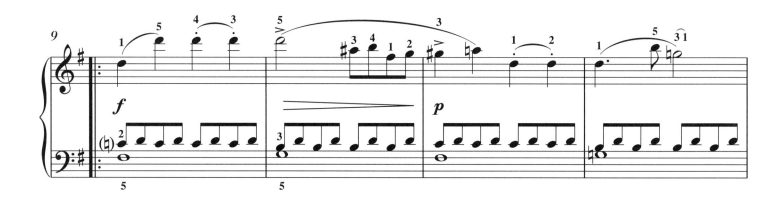

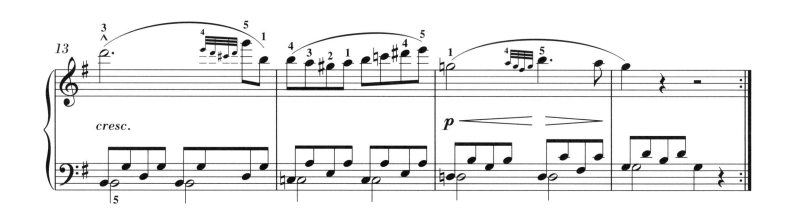

78.

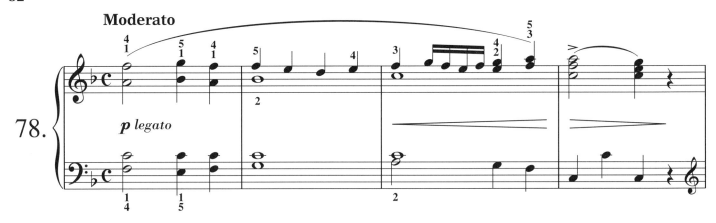

Allegretto à l'hongroise

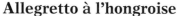

82.

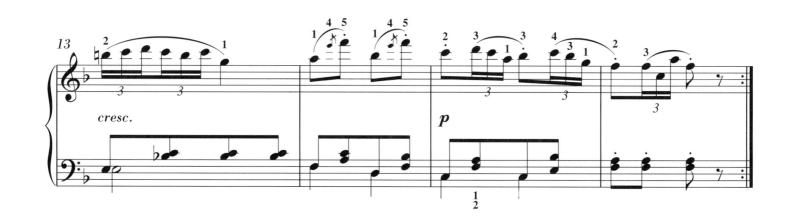

Allegro

83.

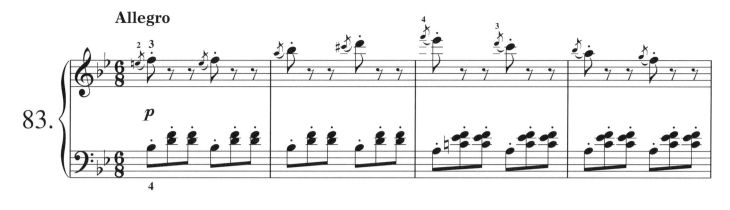

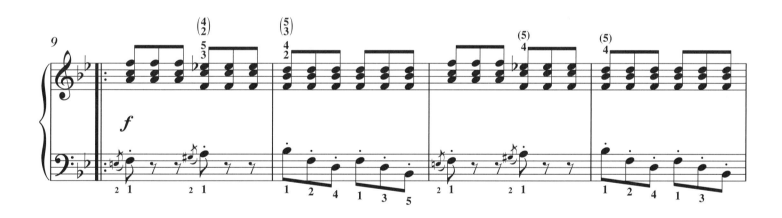

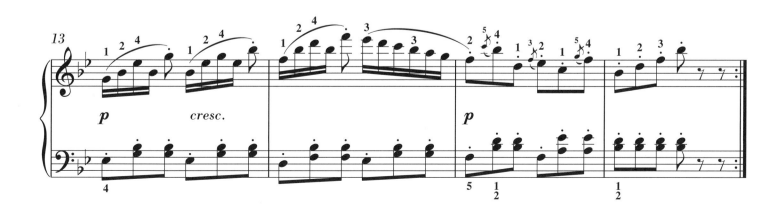

Allegretto

87.

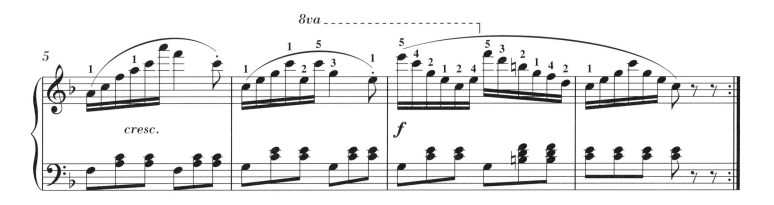

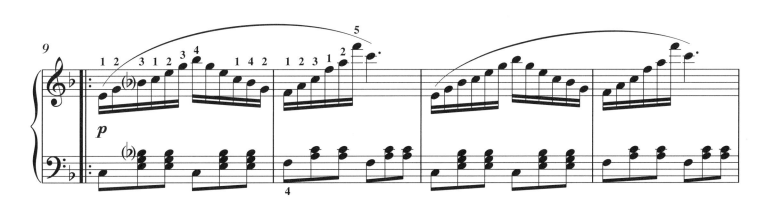

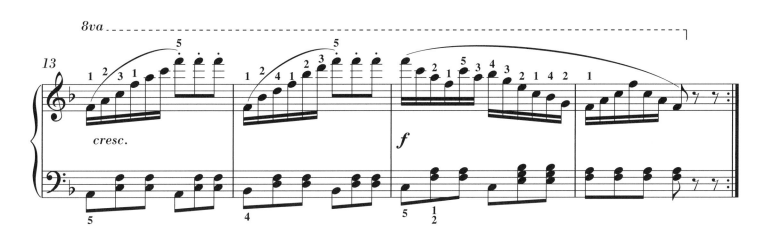

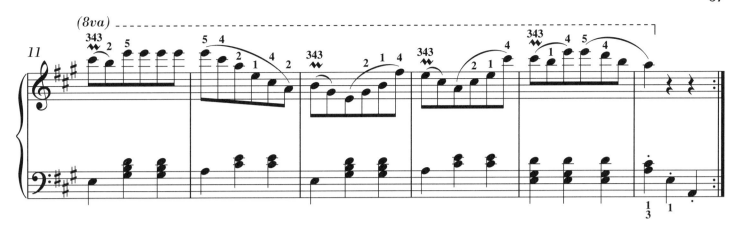

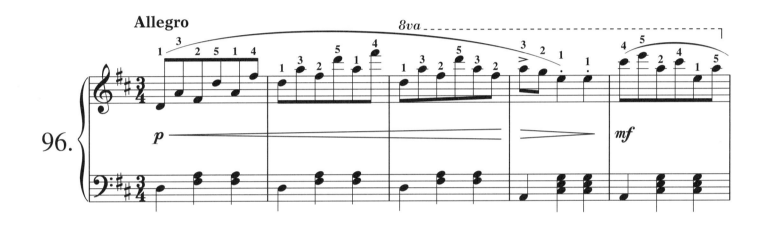

96.

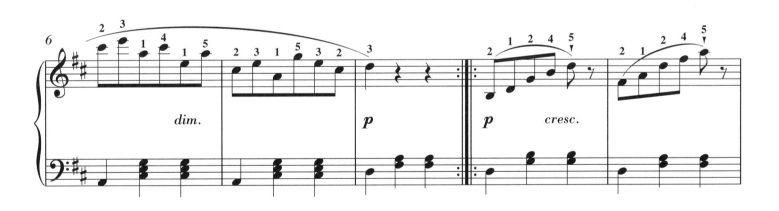

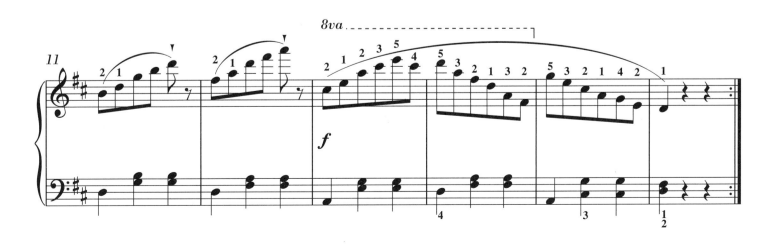

100.

ABOUT THE EDITOR
MATTHEW EDWARDS

Dr. T. Matthew Edwards is a musician of many facets. As a pianist, he has been hailed by critics for his "...considerable talent...honest musicianship, and a formidable technique." His performances have taken him throughout the United States and to Asia, appearing as recitalist, guest artist, concerto soloist, and collaborative artist. His competition winnings include the Grand Prize in the Stravinsky Awards International Competition, and First Prize in the Music Teachers National Association National Collegiate Finals. He has previously served as part-time faculty at several colleges, including the Peabody Conservatory of Music in Baltimore, and full-time as Assistant Professor of Music at Anne Arundel Community College (AACC) in Maryland. Currently, he is Associate Professor of Music and Director of Keyboard Studies at Missouri Western State University. As a lecturer, he has been featured at the National Conference of the Music Teachers National Association, the World Piano Pedagogy Conference, and at the state conventions of the Maryland, Missouri, and Texas Music Teacher's Association. He also serves on the editorial committee for American Music Teacher magazine. As a composer, he has had major works premiered in Chicago, Salt Lake City, and the Baltimore area, and is a contributing author for the Hal Leonard Student Piano Library. As a conductor and coach, Dr. Edwards has served as the rehearsal pianist/coach for the Annapolis Opera, and musical director for Opera AACC. He lives in Kansas City, Missouri with his wife, Kelly, and their three children, Audrey, Jackson, and Cole.

www.thomasmatthewedwards.com